ENGLISH CHILDREN'S COSTUME

English Children's Costume

Since 1775

Drawn and Described by
IRIS BROOKE

With an Introduction by
JAMES LAVER

Adam and Charles Black Limited

FIRST PUBLISHED 1930
REPRINTED 1935, 1949, 1958, 1965, 1978
A. & C. BLACK LTD
35 BEDFORD ROW, LONDON WC1R 4JH
© A. & C. BLACK LTD

ISBN 0 7136 0160 4

PRINTED IN GREAT BRITAIN BY TINDAL PRESS LTD.

INTRODUCTION

IT is no accident that the third quarter of the eighteenth century is the period when the costume of children begins to be distinguishable from that of their elders. In previous ages children had not been looked upon as children, but as incomplete and inferior men and women, wicked by natural impulse and not yet capable of restraining their inevitable tendency to evil by the help of reason and experience. But towards the end of the eighteenth century the rigour of theological dogma had broken down. The doctrine of Original Sin gave place to the notion that " man was born free, and is now everywhere in chains." Man came to be looked upon as a radiant being spoiled by civilisation. His faults were the faults of the world in which he lived, his virtues were all his own.

The results of such a doctrine were both good and evil, and the impulse which induced Rousseau to glorify the noble savage and Marie Antoinette to play at being a milkmaid led inevitably to many incongruous but connected things : a new humanitarianism, a new sentimentality, the reformation of prisons, the abolition of slavery, and the deification of the child.

The notion that children are necessarily better than their elders we need not believe, especially since Freud and his friends have let us into the secret of the awful things that children think ; but the belief that they are different is surely pure gain. If the distinction has been blurred in our own day it is less because children are expected to behave like adults than because adults are so willing to behave like children. The modern passion for sport of all kinds, whatever its benefits, is essentially part of the victory of the child. The early eighteenth-century child could not play in comfort because he was dressed like his father in periwig, long coat, and sword ; the twentieth-century man, when *he* wishes to play, is compelled to dress like his son. Indeed, until the recent, and perhaps temporary, reaction towards longer skirts, there was a general tendency to make the dress of adults of both sexes more and more like the dress of

This tendency has made itself felt ever since there was a special children's dress at all. As Miss Brooke points out (and her charming drawings tell the same tale), boys were wearing trousers for several decades before their fathers thought of following their example, and little girls had something approaching an Empire dress before the Empire itself came into existence. The modern habit of clothing children very scantily has not been without its effect on the clothes of adults, especially those of women.

The influence, however, has not been all one way. Children's clothes, like those of their parents, follow the fashion, but with a difference, the form of which varies with the attitude to the child. When it is looked upon as a kind of doll, it is clothed in the current fashion fantasticated into a kind of fancy dress ; when it is looked upon as a healthy young animal it is dressed in the current fashion simplified into a kind of sports costume.

Children's fashions react more quickly to outside influences than those of their elders. That is their value, as a channel through which modifications can enter. But it is, at least, curious that parents should be willing to announce their political or patriotic opinions in the dress of their offspring, when they would never dream of doing so in their own attire. The naval competition, for example, of the period before the War was faithfully reflected in the dress of multitudes of little English—and German—boys. For those with a taste for such speculations the present volume will offer abundant material, but those who have not will find, in Miss Brooke's delicate drawings and accurate descriptions, the guidance they desire for theatrical production or for "fancy dress." For the accuracy of her detail, Miss Brooke's previous work is a sufficient guarantee, and the drawings themselves are their own best recommendation.

JAMES LAVER.

AUTHOR'S PREFACE

THE earliest record of a definite costume for children is about 1770 or 1775. Before that time children were dressed in exactly the same manner as their parents. The unsuitability of the extreme fashions of the past for small folk weighed not at all on the shoulders of their parents. As they had been dressed, so should their children ; what was good enough when they were young was surely good enough now. Unfortunately an attitude which the older generation has always been rather prone to adopt.

At some time between these two dates an unknown person of fashion decided in a moment of enlightenment that wigs, flowered waistcoats, tight knee-breeches, high heels, and tricorn hats were not altogether suitable for her small sons ; in several paintings of the period we see little boys in long trousers, rather loose, and with low necks to their short coats or shirts, a fashion which soon became the universal wear for the small boys of the time. This is an instance of the child leading the mode, for long trousers had been worn by little boys for almost forty years before they became definitely the fashion for their fathers.

Until the beginning of the nineteenth century little girls were dressed almost identically with their mothers, except that their costume was usually somewhat simpler, and of course the extreme hairdressing fashions of 1785–95 were not inflicted upon children.

I. B.

1775

OF the three costumes on the page overleaf the girl's dress is, perhaps, the quaintest. It is exceedingly difficult to find the exact dates of costumes earlier than about 1790—the time of the first fashion paper in England, and often even in the dated portraits the sitter wears a " picture frock " designed by the artist for the occasion. This particular costume, however, is to be found in two or three paintings of the period, among them Reynolds' famous " Collina." It was a style of dress probably adopted by. the working people at a time when flowing satins and velvets reigned supreme in the houses of the nobility.

The little suit on the right is also taken from a painting by Reynolds, one which may probably claim to be the earliest record of children's costume. The painting is of Viscount Althorp, and was done at some time between 1770 and 1775. When we consider the extravagances of costume affected by the men of the period, the macaronis and exquisites, it is almost incredible to imagine how their children came to be dressed with such charming simplicity.

1775—1795

DURING the next twenty years the traditional long-skirted dress makes its last stand against the new short "Empire" frock of childish simplicity. There is a gradual decline of the former mode as the new style comes more and more into public favour, until at long last, in 1795, the time-honoured traditions are broken and the shorter skirt rules the day. But the revolution is not a drastic one. There are still many examples of ankle length dresses, although the majority were several inches shorter.

Now that shoes are visible, the square-toed and buckled shoes of the later eighteenth century give place to a much lighter type of slipper, similar to the heel-less dancing pumps of to-day.

Boys' suits change little during the next quarter-century, save for a slight variation in the arrangement of sashes and collars.

(see overleaf)

1775

1795

TO the French Revolution goes the honour of changing the extreme fashions of the century. For many years the manufacture of silks had been one of France's staple industries, but this was entirely ruined by the ravages of the Revolution. Paris, quick to realise her power as a leader of fashion, had therefore decreed that printed calicoes and loosely woven cottons should take the place of the silks and velvets of a few years before. These materials were still to be procured by the wealthy, but the prices asked and paid were exorbitant.

In consequence, we see the dresses changing to suit the fabrics. Slowly skirts become shorter and less full, and dainty lawns, gauzes, organdies, percales, and other cotton materials are woven with charming sprig designs and spot patterns to relieve the simplicity of the material. These transparent tissues are frequently worn over a coloured calico slip.

This is the period which Kate Greenaway so charmingly illustrated. Colours are less crude than they have been in recent years, and children are usually seen in either white or pastel shades.

Sashes, fichus, and mob-caps play a leading part in the child's wardrobe and appear on every occasion.

1800

WITH the beginning of a new century, a slight change is noticeable in small boys' suits. The little coat is now often worn open down the front, showing a white frilled shirt underneath. The long trousers are still buttoned on to the shirt, well up above the waist.

Older boys wear tail-coats of the same cut as their fathers', with flowered waistcoats and cravats, and we see them in both knee-breeches and long trousers.

Little girls are still wearing the slightly loose dress, with frilled collar and a frill at the bottom of the sleeve, but the year 1800 marks the birth of the " Empire " dress, cut with a yoke and the skirt gathered on just below the arm-pits.

Hats and bonnets are usually made in chip-straw. The bonnet shape is actually derived from tying the hat under the chin ; as this fashion increased in popularity the back of the brim was cut away to give the wearer more freedom of movement, and the crown was gradually pushed farther to the back of the head until the front brim encircled the face.

1800—1805

SIMPLE and dainty little muslin, gauze, and percale frocks are the fashion now for several years. White and pale shades are most often seen, though coats and cloaks are usually made in darker colours.

All the girls' dresses are cut on the same pattern—a short, tight bodice, with a long skirt slightly gathered on to it. The only way in which a dress could be made individual was by means of the collar and sleeves. We see both long and short sleeves, and both usually have a small puff at the shoulder. Collars are frilled and goffered, so that sometimes they resemble a tiny ruffle.

Bonnets are made with large soft brims and tiny crowns, and tie under the chin.

Little boys have their hair cut short, and still wear the long trousers buttoning just under the arms on to a blouse. Nearly all blouses have short sleeves, and frequently tiny jackets are worn over them; these too often have short sleeves. The throat is rarely covered, and there are all manner of neck-lines.

About 1803 arrives the first little girl to wear long pantaloons, or trousers. This fashion, however, is not taken up for some years to come, though from time to time a few children appear in them, before they eventually become a general feature of the dress itself.

1805—1810

A S a result of the excessive curling and crimping to which
hair has been subjected at the end of the last century,
fashion flies off at a tangent once more, and demands that
the hair be cut short.

From 1805 to 1810 there are several variations from the
straight little bodices and yokes. Cape collars, worn on
dresses and often on coats, are exceedingly fashionable, and
one or two dresses are cut straight from the shoulders without any yoke. A quaint example of this style is seen on
the child at the left of the lower group. It is of magyar
cut, with a bishop sleeve gathered on just above the elbow.
The little dress next to it has the skirt attached straight to
the yoke in the front, and gathered slightly at the back ;
the plaid sash, crossed over the bodice and tied at the back,
gives a fashionable touch to an otherwise simple dress.

Several new styles in hats and bonnets are coming into
fashion.

Boys are wearing much the same styles of clothes as in the
past decade, though now we often see a striped waistcoat.
The smaller boy in the upper group is dressed in much the
same manner as his sisters, except that in his case pantaloons
are always worn and the dress is often above the knees.

1810

A RATHER quaint little dress is seen here on the elder sister. It is made in white percale—a closely woven fabric much used in France at this time—and has a line of blue braid or ribbon round the edge of the jumper-like top. A pale blue scarf is worn with it and tied loosely round the neck in one or two loop knots.

The little boy's trousers are made of jonquille-coloured lawn, and are worn with a white organdie blouse that has tiny cuffs turned back with the jonquille lawn. Slippers of the same shade give a fashionable finish.

The baby on the right is wearing a dress which might have been worn by either a boy or a girl. It is made in a pinky mauve shade of percale, and has tiny frills of white gauze, and a white gauze sash.

Very small children rarely wear shoes or slippers of any kind, but the older ones usually · have their shoes in the same shade as their dresses or suits, and they are frequently made of kid.

The costumes of this particular period are among the most charming in history ; not only are they dainty in the extreme, but they allow a tremendous amount of freedom to their young wearers—a point which, apparently, was not considered in the least from about 1825 until the beginning of the present century.

1810—1815

FASHION strikes several new notes during the next
five years.   The first little boy's costume is very
quaint, the collar giving the effect of the starched front of
a modern dress-shirt!   It is made in double organdie and
has several rows of tucks on the shoulders.   The top stands
up round the throat in the same manner as the collars worn
by the men of this period.

The next suit is similar to the engineers' overalls of to-day ;
suits of this type are commonly worn, with both long and
short sleeves.   Older boys usually wear suits with a military
air, frequently decorated with braid designs on both coat
and trousers.   The high-necked shirt is exceedingly fashionable, and starched and frilled collars give a smart finish to
these suits.

The fashion for little girls has changed hardly at all, but
we see one or two new notes in decoration.   The small
sleeve gathered up in the shoulder, for instance, and the
new square-cut neck-line.

The dress at the left of the lower drawing is something
quite new in style.   The little frilled collar is tied in front
with a plaited cord hanging down almost to the bottom of
the dress.   Here the hair is done up into a small knot on
top, though probably it is an eccentric style and rarely seen.

Short hair is still the vogue.

1 8 1 5 — 1 8 2 0

ONE or two slight changes are now noticeable. Dresses are getting slightly fuller; though still drawn rather tightly across the front, they fall in deep folds at the back. The low square neck is still fashionable.

The military touch in boys' costume, a notable feature, is due, of course, to the influence of the recent wars. We still find the low-necked velvet suit with a lace collar, and sash, a style of dress that is so often seen in paintings of the period.

Hair is being worn perhaps a trifle longer; now we frequently see curls reaching to the shoulders. Top hats and tiny straw ones are often worn by the small boy.

At the right of the lower group is a quaint little suit, probably a court costume, taken from a portrait of Napoleon's son in 1817. It is made in white satin, an exceedingly expensive material at this time, and has a blue silk sash and blue embroidery. It is worn apparently over a kilt and long silk stockings, and is on the whole more reminiscent of the costume of a sixteenth-century page than anything worn during the nineteenth century.

1820

A TIGHTLY fitting, double-breasted little coat made in green broadcloth, with a tiny velvet stand-up collar at the back, and two rows of buttons beginning at the shoulders, is seen here over a white lawn blouse with a ruffle collar, that resembles what is now known as the Toby frill. At this period more little boys are dressed in this sort of suit than in any other.

The girl is wearing a simple dress made in pink gauze, with embroidery at the hem, and a narrow ribbon edging the neck and sleeves. The skirt is quite loose, and perhaps a trifle fuller than the skirts seen on the last page.

The hair is cut in the fashionable manner, with one curl trained to stand up slightly from the parting, and the rest curling almost to the shoulders.

The little boy on the right is wearing a straight little garment tied under the arms with a narrow white ribbon, and reaching just below the knee. Tiny turn-back collar and cuffs, and plain white pantaloons, complete his simple suit.

1820—1825

BETWEEN the years 1820 and 1825 comes the dawn of a new epoch in the history of costume.

The filmy fabrics, so popular during the last quarter of a century, have been replaced by heavier materials, frequently patterned, and in deeper shades.

The clinging skirt is no longer possible in these new materials, and by 1824 all trace of the " Empire " costume has disappeared. Skirts become fuller and shorter, the normal waist-line is once more the vogue, usually emphasized by a tight belt or sash.

Pantaloons play an important part in the costume of all well-dressed girls. They are designed to match each small frock, and dangle around the ankles of their little owners for the next twenty or thirty years.

The dress of the small boy is changing. Tunics are now frequently to the knee, and quite full ; the tight belt at the waist gives an entirely new silhouette. The trousers underneath the tunic are often tucked and frilled as elaborately as those worn by their sisters.

Older boys adopt the costume worn by their fathers, except that their jackets are still short—without tails—and the cravat is not often worn.

1825—1830

A T the left of the upper group is a charming frock of
1826, fashioned in pale blue silk, and covered with
white gauze. It retains something of the simplicity of the
" Empire " dress, with the added charm of fullness : it is
a pity that such a delightful fashion could not have remained
for a few more years, but it was purely transitional, and by
1828 simplicity has gone, irretrievably lost in an avalanche
of extremes.

Hats become larger and larger, and are over-burdened with
ribbon and flowers.

Skirts grow fuller and fuller, braided, tucked, and rouched.
Bodices are tight, often with layers of pleats tightly sewn
into the waistband. The leg-o'-mutton sleeve appears for the
first time. The plaited collar, tied at the throat and standing
up round the face, is greatly worn.

Among this medley of incongruous costumes we find
perhaps two or three charming dresses, shadows of the
future, or reflections of the past. A period of revolutionary
ideas has been reached, and fashions, as they always have
done and always will do, have flown to the opposite extreme.

Small boys are dressed in a more feminine manner ; long
curls have replaced the short manly cut of a few years ago.
We see an extraordinary cap or hat of the time, of the tam-
o'-shanter style, unbelievably large. The chimney-pot hat is
also very popular.

1830

BY 1830 the apex of foolishness has been reached.

Hats have never been so large, and probably never so uncomfortable. Imagine the plight of a small wearer of one such cartwheel of straw, festooned with flowers and ribbon, afraid of a puff of wind which might unbalance it from its precarious hold! Or worse still, the bonnet of this time—large and overwhelmingly bedecked, no wonder that strings had to be firmly fastened under the little chins of the wearers, and the weight must have been tremendous.

The walking dress on the right is made in red velvet, with the bodice pleated from the shoulders to the belt. The upper part of the sleeve resembles an inflated balloon, while the lower part is so tight that it has to be buttoned up.

The boy's dress is perhaps a trifle simpler, though the collar is surmounted by a starched and pleated frill of cambric, which must have been a continual source of annoyance to its possessor.

Here also we see the first appearance of the rather hackneyed form of headgear of the last century, the small boy's peaked cap with the tassel, dear to so many artists of the Victorian era.

Organdie and gingham played an important part in the making of dresses and suits of this time, partly on account of their stiffness.

1830—1835

THE first year or two of the 'thirties still hold to extremes. The children of a hundred years ago parade
solemnly before us, their fashionably stiffened dresses sadly
restricting their movements, their bonnets so large that they
must be placed well to the back of the head, their pantaloons
flapping over the tops of their shoes.

But by 1833 fashions have become less extreme. The
skirt is almost a crinoline, though, so far, no hoops have
come into being. The skirt is held out by stiffly corded
petticoats, probably four or five, starched almost to
cracking-point. The leg-o'-mutton sleeve is almost universally worn. We still see the small puff sleeves on several
dresses, and sometimes the long tight sleeve with the puff
from elbow to shoulder.

The tremendous hats and bonnets of the last year or so
have been supplanted by the smaller bonnet—not actually
poke, but rather like a sun-bonnet in style.

Collars are frequently so large that they stand out several
inches beyond the shoulders of their wearers, giving an
extraordinarily wide effect, reminiscent of the dress worn
at the time of Henry VIII. This is the mode for both boys
and girls. It is extraordinary how this particular fashion
of enlarging the shoulders and sleeves, and tightening the
waist, has become so popular from time to time. We see it
again in a more modified style between the years 1880 and
1890.

1835—1840

HERE are several changes in style.

The leg-o'-mutton sleeve is still worn in various forms by little boys, and occasionally by their sisters, but the short tight sleeve is more popular. It is usually ornamented with frills, rouching or tucks, and rarely reaches as far as the elbow. Mittens, frequently made of black silk, are all the rage.

Large collars no longer deform the shoulders of the children. Usually the neck is cut fairly low, with a small frill. Pelisses have become a very important article of attire, and are usually made of cashmere, frequently embroidered, and with a frill all round the edge.

Bonnets are in the charming cottage style, and usually are ornamented with ribbon, and occasionally with feathers. The hair is almost always parted in the middle and drawn into a bow of ribbon or imitation flower at each side of the face. The centre parting was a style set by Queen Victoria, and rigidly adhered to during the first twenty years or so of her reign.

Little boys are still wearing tunics in the style of the last six or seven years. But the frilled cambric blouse is also very popular, and trousers are tighter at the ankle and exceedingly full at the hips. Plaid and check are very fashionable for the small boy.

1840

HERE is a quaint example of the coat of the period ; buttoned tightly to the waist, it falls unfastened to the hem of the dress, allowing for the extreme fullness of the frock beneath. It is trimmed with white swansdown, the most popular trimming of the time.

The little pink dress is made of glacé silk, with flowers of organdie, and a belt of red velvet. The bonnet to match is of red velvet, lined and trimmed with pink silk.

The little boy on the right is dressed in a typical suit of the time. The trousers have once more resumed their original cut ; the queer fashion of gathering at the hips and fitting tightly at the ankles has not lasted very long. Short black coats worn with linen collars are very popular. Plaid trousers and Glengarry caps are considered exceedingly smart.

The tiny figure on the left is in a dress designed for the small boy, for at this period small boys usually wear petticoats, until they have attained the age of five years, and they frequently appeared in the same frocks as their sisters. The large black hat is made of beaver, trimmed with an ostrich feather and blue cockade.

1840—1845

DURING the next five years there are very few new
ideas. We see again the little boys in long trousers
buttoned on to short coats, or long tunics worn over embroidered pantaloons or long trousers. Hair is frequently
cut short at the ear—the Buster Brown cut, as it was then
called.

Little girls still come out in the charming poke-bonnet,
the short cape, and the ankle-length pantaloons. The skirt
length varies considerably, but the longer ones are generally
the more fashionable. The skirts are not so heavily frilled
as they have been recently, though tucks are still fashionable.
The bodice is the most important part of the dress, and
collars are large and varied in style. The apron is still a
very popular accessory.

The dress worn by the tallest girl at the top of the page
is made of taffeta, which was then called glacé silk, and
trimmed with the same material gathered on to a narrow
ribbon of contrasting colour. The whole of the trimming
is edged with an inch-wide lace—probably hand-made, as
lace-making was one of the most popular occupations of the
contemporary ladies of fashion.

1845—1850

THE first dress here, proudly displayed by its wearer, shows us a new style in neck lines, a fashion adopted from the court dress of the period, and followed for evening wear during the next twenty years or more.

Here also is the first example for many years of a dress with short pantaloons, barely reaching as far as the skirt itself, which is decidedly shorter. This is a fashion much adopted for party frocks, the long pantaloons still being worn for day-time and ordinary wear. This shortened style is also worn by small boys, the trousers being cut to a few inches below the knees, and socks visible for the first time. Sailor suits of varied forms are greatly favoured, and plaid and checks are universally fashionable.

Boys frequently wear their hair long, until they reach the age thought suitable for them to go into trousers. It is then often cut to the shoulders for several years, before it is eventually cut short.

There is a quaint caricature of Scottish costume in the dress of the younger boy in the lower group. The plaid kilt is worn over white cambric trousers with embroidered edges, plain stockings, and buttoned boots. A black velvet coat, with Eton collar, bow tie, and white silk shirt, completes this strange suit.

1850

SKIRTS have become too large to be supported entirely by corded petticoats and whaleboning: the crinoline has arrived—a weird article of apparel resembling a flexible wire cage.

The small girl wears a quaint little sun-bonnet, and one of the new short coats cut straight to the waist, with about six inches flared to fit over the top of the skirt. And she has the new bell-shaped sleeve, showing at the wrist the tiny puff belonging to the dress underneath.

The older girl has her hair dressed in the modish style. It is done up in a loose chignon at the back of the neck, and a chenille net is worn over the whole. She is wearing a very fashionable dress with a three-tiered white tarlatan skirt and a short-sleeved velvet coatee. She is also wearing short pantaloons barely visible beneath her excessively full skirts.

The boy's costume is typical of the time. He wears a blue and white plaid gingham blouse and fashionably cut trousers of some heavy material with a silk braid stripe down the outside of the leg. His stockings are hand-knitted and are striped with blue.

This is perhaps one of the first appearances of the striped stocking, which remained for several years the fashion for children of all ages and of both sexes. Probably as the leg had been discreetly covered for so many years, it was difficult at first to become used to an unadorned calf, and stripes were therefore introduced with the idea of decorating the rudely exposed leg.

1850—1855

THE reign of the poke-bonnet is over, dethroned by a large flapping wheel of straw with a minute crown, and worn well on the back of the head and secured under the chin with ribbons. These hats are usually made of leghorn, and have a small ribbon tied round the crown, its ends falling down the back.

Elastic-sided boots are the most modish style of footgear. Not only are they adopted for street wear, but we see several examples in coloured cloth with shiny patent leather toe-caps and heels, worn at parties and on other dressy occasions.

Nearly all little girls are wearing the new bell-shaped sleeve, frequently with dainty lacy frills showing at the wrist. Morning and walking dresses are high at the throat, but evening and party frocks are still cut excessively low. Often the tiny sleeve has a ribbon passed through it and tied in a bow on the shoulder ; this keeps it from slipping up at every movement. Little shaped jackets and coats are very becoming, and are frequently trimmed with fur. Skirts are exceedingly full and are mostly made with several deep frills.

Another fresh mode of hairdressing has been introduced for girls—the wearing of plaits over the ears, and a small wreath of imitation flowers fastened to the plaits.

Boy's costume has not changed a great deal. Here is one example of the check tweed suit, and a queer little hat resembling a flattened "bowler," with a wavy brim. Another style is the rather military cap with a stiffened peak of patent leather.

1855—1860

DURING the next few years children's costume makes many and varied changes. Boys' knees are visible for the first time, and occasionally we even get a peep of their small sisters' knees, discreetly camouflaged with frilled knickers and striped stockings.

The first suit on this page might almost be worn to-day. It is carried out in yellow nankeen, with a black patent-leather belt and a straw sailor-hat. The suit directly below has a new shape in trousers, gathered into a tight band and fastened a few inches above the knee. The next little boy is dressed on much the same lines as his father, whilst the third—the little one—has an entirely new type of headgear.

Crinolines are getting larger and larger, and they are frequently seen with a bunched-up skirt worn over the other, adding considerably to the effect of size. Braid is the most popular trimming for the bottom of a skirt. We still see one or two examples of the long pantaloons, though the shorter ones are more frequently worn.

Hats for girls get smaller and vary greatly in shape, from the one that resembles an inverted wash-basin, to a small flat cap worn well on the front of the head, like that of the smallest boy.

The hair is dressed very often in the chenille net, and we also see a new style of dragging the hair right away from the face and exposing the ears.

1860

BY 1860 long pantaloons have definitely gone out of fashion. In their place are loose drawers reaching an inch or so below the dress.

Here is a fashionable style of evening dress, made in white illusion, an exceedingly fashionable material resembling a fine tulle. The low neck-line is accentuated by bows of pink ribbon on the shoulders. This particular dress has no sleeves at all.

The little girl on the right is wearing one of the new *panier* dresses, made in purple velvet and trimmed with yellow braid and deep cream lace collar and cuffs. Her hair is also dressed in a new style—brushed straight off the face and held back with a narrow velvet ribbon going round the head under the hair and tied in front with a small bow.

The young gentleman in the centre has a new style of suit, of black velvet, with linen collar and cuffs edged with point lace. His trousers are another new pattern—they are made in a design very similar to the plus-fours of to-day. The heavy fringe and long curls is a style of hairdressing for boys that we frequently see during the next few years, though it never became remarkably popular.

1860—1865

THE crinoline has reached impossible dimensions, and with its increased size the skirt becomes shorter and still shorter, giving an absurd mushroom effect.

Funny little cloaks, with hoods and tiny capes over the shoulders, are very much worn. Braid plays the most important part in the trimmings on little girls' frocks, and many curious designs appear round the hems of the skirts, coats, and the edges to the still popular bell-shaped sleeves.

Bodices are not so tightly fitted as they have been recently ; we frequently see them pouched over the top of the skirt, the actual waistband still being fairly tight.

The " plus-four " type of leg-wear for boys is exceedingly fashionable, and the belted tunic that has been the mode for so many years is now rarely seen. Nearly all children wear striped stockings and elastic-sided boots of ankle height.

Tiny hats and caps still perch on the tops of little heads, and feathers are a fashionable adornment. The hair drawn back from the forehead and hanging long and straight down the back, the full, short skirts, with rows of braid adorning the hem, the striped stockings and small patent-leather, ankle-strapped slippers, recall vividly Tenniel's apt illustrations for *Alice in Wonderland.*

1865—1870

THE chignons and chenille nets are no longer seen The hair is usually worn quite loose, and, if possible, brushed into curls. The fringe has made its first appearance for many years, though by many it is looked upon with disfavour.

By 1868 the crinoline, having reached the largest possible dimensions, is taken out and left to rust on the dust-heap. The skirt, robbed of its chief support, slowly subsides like a pricked balloon, and rests once more on the corded petticoat. With the waning of the crinoline, several other fashions also disappear. The *panier* effect, so modish for a few years, is seen no more.

Bell-sleeves have been supplanted by tightly-fitting sleeves with cuffs, or gathered in four or five puffs from shoulder to wrist—a fashion which we have not seen for many years. The puff sleeves at the shoulder are still worn a great deal by small children for party frocks.

For the small boy, the sailor suit is adopted, and several strange patterns are derived from it. Short coats with long trousers, still frequently plaid, are as fashionable as the baggy calf-length trousers, usually worn with the longer coat. Top-hats, small, round caps, and flat straw hats are most often seen.

1870

WE have entered upon an era of hideous colours. Dark and heavy materials with large patterns, stripes and plaids, have supplanted the lighter ones of the crinoline period.

Hats have assumed the dimensions of a small plate, and are balanced on the front of the head and held in position either by elastic under the hair or by ribbons.

An exceedingly odd suit for boys is seen here, made in dull red plush and trimmed with squirrel, with a quaint " mortar-board " style of head-dress, also trimmed with fur. This particular costume is said to be suitable for the young gentleman of from six to twelve years. Let us hope that the young gentleman thought it suitable ! I find it difficult to think of anything less practical.

The little girl in blue is wearing one of the fashionable cross-over fichus, a mode which became the craze for a year or two.

The child with the doll has a complicated garment composed of bottle-green merino, with book-muslin fichu, sash and apron-front, trimmed with two rows of braid and a tiny edging of crochet. The skirt is of striped piqué and is supported by many starched petticoats and the still fashionable corded petticoat.

1870—1875

THE fringe has become definitely fashionable, and heavy, straight fringes are worn by boys and girls alike. Little boys are wearing their hair long again; it is extraordinary how, from time to time, we see boys with long curls, and in a few years' time off they come—and none but the shorn are smart.

All sorts of skirts are seen during these years, each with some added material or trimming, in an endeavour to make up for the recently lost crinoline. Mostly they have over-skirts, frequently bundled up behind; but we see them quilted, heavily braided, and paniered, and, when nothing else avails, a large sash is tied at the back to add zest to the outline.

Every garment has plenty of braid and buttons. Bodices are higher at the throat and rarely have collars, the neck usually being finished with a tiny frill or just a braid binding. Sailor collars are often worn on coats, and a striped singlet is very smart.

Hats perch either forward over the eyes or on the top of the head; they are still small, and often there is more decoration than hat. Small shoulder capes, sometimes made of fur, are worn over the coat, but the long cloak of a year or two ago has vanished. Muffs are a fashionable adjunct to the well-dressed child.

1875—1880

THE years between 1875 and 1880 see many changes.
Fashion demands that the back of the skirt be the
most important part of the dress, so by some method or
other it must be exaggerated.   We see, therefore, layers of
frills down the back, large bows of material, and frequently
an overskirt in a contrasting colour, draped tightly across
the front and gathered up at the back into a little bunch,
to which a large bow of ribbon or of the same material is
attached.   The apron effect is very popular ; so also are
large cuffs, and we see again sleeves that bulge at the shoulder.

Hats are getting larger again.   Starched muslin hats with
layers of goffered frills, decorated with flowers and ribbon,
are very fashionable.   We also see small straw hats with
large bows of ribbon in the front, and several different kinds
of tam-o'-shanter, for the boy as well as the girl.   Heavy
fringes and long curls, or plaits, are most worn.

Dark colours, such as puce, purple, bottle-green, plum,
navy, and scarlet are very popular, and heavy materials—
merino, oatmeal cloth, hopsack, alpaca, cashmere, serge,
and so on—are very much used.

Boys usually appear in sailor suits, with reefer-coats, or in
velvet suits with knee-breeches buttoning tightly below the
knee.

1880

O N this page is seen a favourite type of dress for the small girl, worn a great deal during the next few years. This particular costume is made in scarlet cashmere with a navy blue sash, and trimmed with a white frill round the throat and wrists. The bodice is tight-fitting down to the hips, and the kilted skirt has under it a starched petticoat with all the gathers at the back, which lifts the skirt sufficiently to give the fashionable outline. The sash is long and ties in a large bow at the back. The little cap or hat is made of scarlet velvet with a blue ribbon round it, tied in a large bow in the front.

The boy in the centre wears a type of Norfolk jacket ; in this instance the box-pleat at the back goes right up to the collar of the coat. He is also wearing a " fisher cap " of knitted scarlet wool, reminiscent of the liberty caps of the French Revolution.

The navy blue jersey worn by the other boy is one of the first to be seen adopted for the ordinary child, although jerseys and guernseys have been worn for many years by the fisher folk.

Both boys have the new type of knee-breeches, fitting their legs almost like a skin, and buttoned with two or three buttons below the knee.

1880—1885

THE draped overskirt has become exceedingly fashionable, and is called the " fishwife " style. Practically all the little girls' dresses, which are not made in the pattern described on the last page, are cut in the " fishwife " style. The overskirt is made with the bodice, and the skirt underneath is frequently made of a different material. The overskirt is occasionally seen gathered up in the front as well as the back.

Sometimes a small pad is inserted at the back of the dress to make the skirt stand out more, and sashes or flaps of material usually add to the effect.

Both pleating and frilling are very popular trimmings for the skirt when it is made of the same material as the dress. Sleeves are nearly always tight-fitting from the elbow, but sometimes we see them large and balloon-like at the shoulder. Dresses are high at the throat and rarely have collars—a small frill is the usual mode of finish to the neck of a dress.

Little boys frequently wear the Little Lord Fauntleroy style of costume in black velvet and lace, with a wide sash tied round the waist. The serge suit, with tight-fitting knee-breeches, is also a favourite.

1885—1890

TWEED has become fashionable for the small boy's suit, and we see here a rather hectic example of a rough check, three-piece tweed, worn with an Eton collar and bow tie. Lapels are rarely cut on boys' coats at this time. They are made to fasten at the neck, and usually fall open from there.

Sailor suits of many different styles are still the rage, and a striped singlet is often worn under the blouse. Trousers of all descriptions are worn with these suits, both tight-fitting and baggy, long and short. The fisher-cap and tam-o'-shanter are still popular.

Little girls' dresses are similar to recent fashions, though not quite the same ; the bodice is now usually worn loose, and hangs over the sash or belt. The pad at the back of the dress is out of fashion, and the " fishwife " effect is no longer gained by lifting up an overskirt ; it is usually a shaped sash or apron cut to a slight point in the front and gathered up at the back.

Hats are quite large, with a rather small crown, and are worn at the back of the head. There is also a version of the mob-cap, with a large bow of ribbon in the front. The hair is still cut with a heavy fringe.

1890

THE dress of the 'eighties has vanished, and the bustle
is no more.

A revival of the " Empire " costume is in progress,
brought about by the illustrations of Kate Greenaway, and
we see several tiny children in long, high-waisted dresses,
and long coats with a cape collar. These dresses, however,
appear ridiculous when carried out in the dark and bulky
materials of the 'nineties. Several attempts are made during
the next few years to bring dresses of this kind into more
general use.

With this revival comes once more the fashion for short
hair, though this time it only remains in vogue for a year or
two. The back is cut shorter than the front, and the front
hair well curled.

Smocks are considered very smart for girls, both little and
big, and we see them, with many varying kinds of sleeves,
a great deal during the succeeding years.

The dark red dress is made in serge, with a black patent-
leather belt and white silk frills. Serge is a material very
much worn, and we see the little boy in the centre, also
attired in a serge reefer-coat with a black velvet collar and
black buttons. The cap is also of scarlet serge, with a black
silk ribbon tied round it.

Striped stockings are still occasionally seen, though they
are not generally worn, and buttoned boots are a popular
footwear.

1890—1895

VERY few new styles present themselves during these five years.

Here is an example of the long cape I have described on the previous page, worn with an absurd little cap something like a chef's cap in miniature, perched well to the back of the head. Little girls are beginning to adopt the sailor blouse and reefer-coat, worn with a short pleated skirt. We see an example of this on the little girl in the tam-o'-shanter on the see-saw.

The little boy at the extreme right of the upper group is wearing a tweed cap and suit, with a large soft linen collar and a bow tie. Most of the small children are in dark-coloured velvets, serges, hopsacks, etc.

It is difficult to point to any particular mode as typical of this period, for fashion is again going through a transition stage. Sleeves of various styles are seen. The waist-line is usually at the normal. There are collars of every description, and skirt lengths may vary from the knee to the ankle. Hair is worn either long or short. In fact, almost anything within bounds may be worn and still appear more or less fashionable.

1895—1900

A NEW style of trousers has come into being, known generally as " shorts," since they barely reach to the knee ! White silk shirts with large collars and cuffs are often worn by the little boy.

Highwayman coats and hats are exceedingly fashionable. We frequently see the coats in bottle-green or claret-coloured broadcloth, with a stand-up collar in black velvet, and a black velour tricorn hat. Little boys still wear the Little Lord Fauntleroy suit in black velvet, although it is considered rather effeminate to wear long curls. The coat with the double-cape collar is also a popular fashion for little girls, the collars often with fur round the edge.

A type of bonnet has arrived that is quite new, with a tight-fitting band round the face and the back gathered in, usually carried out in either velvet or satin, and the " brim " frequently embroidered. Hats are usually large, and we often see small children in the starched muslin hats worn a few years ago.

Dresses are still of varying lengths, and little ones often have them almost reaching to their ankles. Frills and lace and embroidery are very fashionable, and frocks are frequently made entirely in embroidered muslin or lawn.

The dull colours of a few years ago have given place to white and cream, which are by far the most fashionable shades for the small child.

1900

IF we turn back and compare these costumes with those of 1800 a remarkable similarity will be seen.

Having passed through a hundred years of ever-changing fashions, witnessing the rise and decline of the crinoline, the birth and death of the bustle, the coming and going of many weird and wonderful fashions, we end up, one hundred years later, a few inches from where we started.

Heavy materials have had their day, and once again children are dressed in pale colours, cream and white, and in decidedly daintier fabrics than they have recently been wearing.

Swiss embroidered muslin, silk, and voile are perhaps the most popular, embroidery playing a great part in the fashionable child's dress. We rarely see little girls in anything but white, and often embroidery is the only decoration. Sashes in pastel shades give the solitary touch of colour.

The little boy is wearing an ivory velvet suit with a silk shirt. He has fashionably short trousers.

The little girl on the right is in a Swiss embroidered voile, with a narrow pale mauve ribbon at the waist. The round neck, with a wide gathered collar, is seen a great deal, and short sleeves come in again—the first appearance of the elbow for some years.

1900—1905

THE fashion for dressing children in white and cream is, if possible, even more prevalent than it has been. Little white frilly muslin and voile frocks, with deep embroidered hems and yokes, white washing silk smocks, cream serge coats, jerseys and kilts, and white drill or duck sailor suits are seen on every occasion.

Stockings are either black, white, or brown; and socks are black, white, navy, and brown.

The schoolgirl, we usually find, is wearing navy blue serge. Her dress is frequently made with a sailor collar and rows of white cotton braid arranged round the hem and cuffs. Sleeves are always shaped with the fullness gathered in on the shoulders, giving a slightly leg-o'-mutton appearance.

She also wears a shiny, stiff straw hat ; usually this has a wide brim, but occasionally the brim is only two or three inches wide, resembling the straw " boater " worn by the undergraduate—in either case equally hard and unyielding and exceedingly uncomfortable.

Occasionally little boys wear black velvet knee-breeches and blouses, with lace collar and cuffs, but the jersey and sailor suit are gradually becoming more and more popular. Eton suits and Norfolk suits are worn usually by the older boy.

1905—1910

MUCH the same style in dress prevails during the next five years. Tiny children are still seen dressed entirely in white, but those over five years of age begin to appear again in pale colours.

Spotted muslins and embroidered Swiss materials still hold their own, but now they are usually worn over a coloured silk slip. Large collars have become very fashionable, and we see them in many different shapes and styles.

Although sleeves are still gathered at the shoulders, they rarely taper to the wrists but remain full all the way to the cuff, which may be any depth from four to five inches to a half-inch frill. Usually the little girls' dresses have a high waist-line with a tiny yoke, but the older girl wears her belt or sash at the normal waist-line.

It is fashionable for socks to reach almost to the knee ; these are called the three-quarter-length socks.

Hair ribbons of all descriptions are worn, and we see several quaint contrivances of elastic and ribbon worn round the head with a bow on each side and the elastic under the hair at the back. Sometimes the ribbon is gathered onto the elastic across the front of the head.

Little boys are wearing the same style of dress as they have done for the last eight or nine years. The knee-length " shorts " are the most popular form of trousers.

1910

ON the left is a rather jolly example of a blue Liberty velvet frock, with green and blue embroidered butterflies at the neck and sleeves. This type of dress is usually worn over a white washing-silk blouse.

The little girl's hair is parted in the middle, and the hair at each side is taken back and tied with a bow on the top of the head.

The boy is dressed in a cream alpaca suit with a square, semi-sailor collar and large pearl buttons down the coat and at the knee. He wears a scarlet patent-leather belt and a white flannel singlet at the throat.

The three smaller children all wear the fashionable three-quarter-length socks.

The elder girl has a dress of pink silk, with the fashionable cape collar and large loose sleeves from the shoulder to the elbow, with a long, tight-fitting cuff. All the smartest children's dresses are embroidered, frequently in the same shade as the dress itself.

Smocks are still very smart for the small child, and the example here is carried out in white washing-silk, smocked at the yoke and wrist with scarlet silk.

1910—1915

BY 1910 the restrictions on colour had been overcome, and once again children are clothed in brilliant and dainty colours, and in other materials than the everlasting serge and muslin of the last ten years.

Although gym-tunics—or drill-dresses, as they were first called—had been worn for sports and games for many years, they did not come into general use for school wear until about 1910 or 1912, and from that date up to the present day most schools have adopted this style as a uniform.

About 1914 the waist-line for children's dresses is seen somewhere about the thighs, with only a few inches of frill or kilt below the belt. This fashion became an absolute fetish and prevailed for several years.

I can testify from personal experience that these dresses were not very comfortable, for often when running or jumping—or sometimes even when sitting down—the tight belt would suddenly split with the strain. Or else, if you had not been too careful in putting the belt through its slots, you would find yourself walking along with the belt round your ankles.

1915—1920

WE still see several children wearing the low waisted dresses, but by 1916 or 1917 once again the skirt is gathered onto a yoke or short bodice considerably above the normal waist-line.

Both dresses and socks are getting, each year, briefer and briefer, so that by 1920 the smartest dressed children often display more bare leg than dress.

All kinds of patterned materials have again become fashionable. Brightly-coloured flowered, spotted and plaid chintzes, gingham, and voiles are used for dainty little summer frocks.

Another sweeping fashion for short hair has set in; it becomes more and more prevalent, until by 1920 it is rare to see any little girls with long hair. With this fashion comes an overpowering tendency for hair ribbons to get larger and larger, and stiff silk ribbons, sometimes 5 or 6 inches wide, and 1¼ yard long, are perched on the tops of little " bobbed " heads. As a result, little girls are often going about without hats.

Boys are wearing tweed flannel and serge suits; jerseys and sailor jumpers are equally smart for the boy or girl.

During the years of the Great War, knitting had become a universal habit, so much so that in 1919, the War being at an end and no more socks, gloves, or scarves needed by the troops, there was a fashion for knitted dresses and jumpers; and it may safely be said that every other child seen during the winters of 1919 and 1920 wore a hand-knitted garment of some sort.